JUVENILE DIABETES

JUVENILE DIABETES

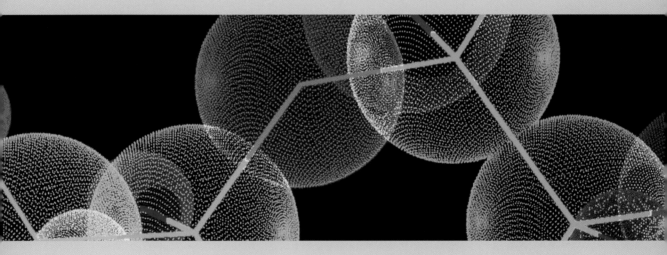

Johannah Haney

BENCHMARK BOOKS

MARSHALL CAVENDISH
NEW YORK

With thanks to Renato N. Mascardo, M.D., FACE, FACP, Assistant Clinical Professor of Medicine, Division of Endocrinology & Metabolism, University of Connecticut School of Medicine, for his expert review of the manuscript.

Benchmark Books
Marshall Cavendish
99 White Plains Road
Tarrytown, New York 10591-9001
www.marshallcavendish.com

Library of Congress Cataloging-in-Publication Data

Haney, Johannah.
Juvenile diabetes / Johannah Haney.
p. cm. — (Health alert)
Includes bibliographical references and index.
ISBN 0-7614-1798-2
1. Diabetes in children—Juvenile literature. 2. Diabetes—Juvenile literature. I. Title. II. Series: Health alert (Benchmark Books)

RJ420.D5H355 2005
616.4'62--dc22
2004005969

Front cover: Instruments and medicine used to maintain proper blood glucose levels
Title page: A computer graphic of a molecule of human insulin

Photo research by Regina Flanagan
Front cover: Digital Vision / Picture Quest
The photographs in this book are used by permission and through the courtesy of:
Photo Researchers, Inc.: A. Pasieka, 2; John M. Daugherty, 9; John Bavosi, 10; Leonard Lessin, 16; Dr. Linda Stannard, UCT, 18; Saturn Stills, 29, 40; E. Young, 30; Steve Horrell, 36; Michael P. Gadomski, 37; James King-Holmes, 43; Charles D. Winters, 45; Sue Ford, 49; SPL, 50; Cnri, 51. *Corbis:* 14, 47 (left); Arthur Beck, 17; Archivo Iconografico, S.A., 21; Hulton-Deutsch Collection, 26; Bettmann, 27, 28, 47 (center), 47 (right); Richard T. Nowitz, 32; ER Productions, 39; Tom & Dee Ann McCarthy, 46; Michael Heron, 52; Jose Luis Pelaez, Inc., 53. *Picture Quest:* Ron Chapple / Thinkstock, 41. *Getty Images:* 35, 44. *Creatas:* 38.

Printed in China
6 5 4 3 2 1

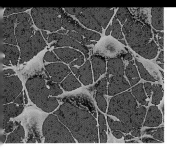

CONTENTS

WHAT IS IT LIKE TO HAVE JUVENILE DIABETES?

When Kathleen was six years old, she was just like other kindergartners. She enjoyed learning new things in school and she loved playing on the swings at recess. But by the end of the school year, Kathleen was thirsty all the time, had to ask the teacher for a lot of bathroom breaks, and sometimes fell asleep during class. Children can often become thirsty and tired, but Kathleen seemed to be thirstier and more tired than other children her age.

Her parents were worried so they took her to the doctor. The doctor examined Kathleen and had her go to the hospital to have some tests done. One of the tests checked Kathleen's **blood glucose**—or the sugar in her bloodstream. Abnormal blood glucose levels are often a sign of juvenile diabetes. When the test results came back, the doctor found out that

Kathleen had juvenile diabetes. This meant that her body had a hard time regulating the sugar levels in her bloodstream.

The doctors and nurses taught Kathleen and her parents about diabetes and showed her how to take care of herself. Kathleen met other children who had diabetes and realized that she was not alone. There were many other people like her out there.

When Kathleen went to school, she had to be careful. Every day she had to check her blood glucose level at least four times, measure everything she ate, exercise for at least half an hour, and take two insulin shots. If Kathleen felt sick at school, she needed to go to the nurse's office. At the nurse's office, they would test Kathleen's blood and adjust her blood glucose level.

As Kathleen grew up, she began to understand her disease better. Kathleen is now in her twenties and has learned how to deal with her diabetes. Following her doctors' orders, she eats the right foods, exercises regularly, carefully monitors her blood glucose levels, and takes her medication. She has found that she can live a normal life with juvenile diabetes. It will always be a part of Kathleen's life, but she has learned that it does not have to be the most important thing in her life.

WHAT IS JUVENILE DIABETES?

In order to function properly, the human body needs energy. This energy comes from the food a person eats. Turning the food into usable energy is a complex process that involves **carbohydrates, glucose,** the **pancreas,** and **insulin.**

Carbohydrates are chemical compounds found in food. Some occur naturally and others are created by people. Simple sugars and starches are carbohydrates. Junk food such as soda, candy, and ice cream have a lot of simple sugars. The sugar was added to make them taste sweet. Food such as fruit, honey, and molasses naturally contains sugar. Starches are found in potatoes, rice, pasta, beans, and grain.

When the human body digests food, it turns carbohydrates into glucose. There is always some glucose in a person's blood. This amount can be measured, and the measurement is called the glucose level. Glucose is then

metabolized—changed—in body cells to make energy. A person needs to have the right glucose level in his or her blood. If there is not enough glucose, the body will not have enough energy. The pancreas—an organ located behind the stomach—aids in metabolizing glucose.

One of the jobs of the pancreas is to produce **hormones**. These are chemicals that help body functions. Some hormones are involved with growth and development. The hormone

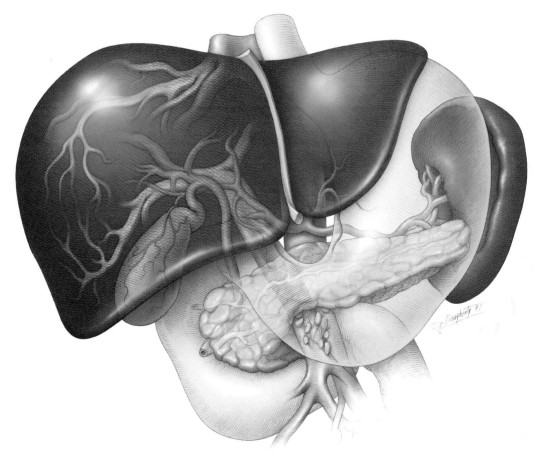

The pancreas—shown here as a pink oblong structure—is part of the digestive system.

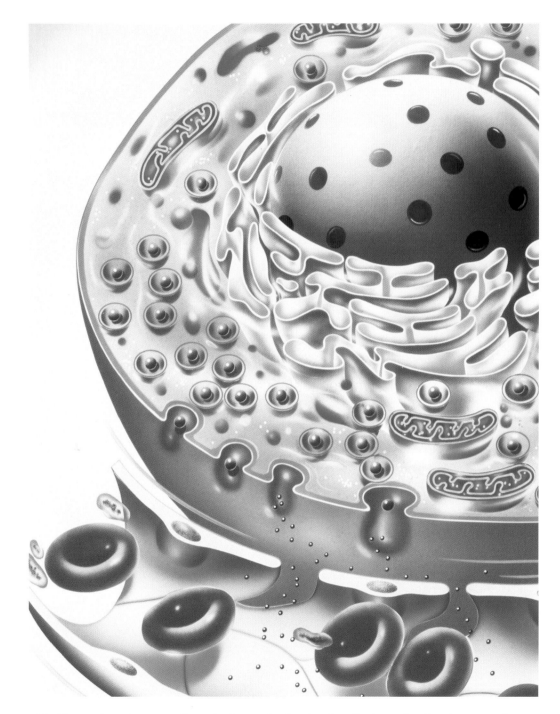

This illustration shows a cell producing and releasing insulin into the bloodstream. The insulin is contained within the granules (small blue balls) which are secreted into the blood.

insulin is produced in the pancreas by special pancreatic cells called **islets of Langerhans.** Insulin helps glucose to enter the body's cells. Once there, the glucose is metabolized and turned into energy. The body needs this energy to move, eat, sleep, grow, and heal.

WHAT GOES WRONG

When a person has diabetes, the pancreas stops making insulin. Without insulin, the glucose in the blood cannot enter the cells. Instead, it stays in the bloodstream. Since blood is not meant to have so much glucose in it, other organs in the body will try to correct the problem. The job of the **kidneys** is to help keep blood and other body fluids clean. The kidneys take the extra glucose in the bloodstream and remove it through urine. The body loses a large volume of fluid through urine. As a result, a person with diabetes (called a diabetic) is very thristy. Diabetics also need to urinate frequently.

Besides building up high glucose levels, the body can also become deprived of energy. Since there is no insulin to help the glucose get into the cells, very little energy is made. The body tries to fix this problem. Fat and protein that have been stored are used to make energy. Fat and protein are usually good sources of energy for the body, but when no carbohy-drates are there to help provide energy, the body must work harder to use the stored protein and fat. All this work is hard on the body. A diabetic might lose weight because the body is using up most of the stored fat for energy.

HYPOGLYCEMIA

Hypoglycemia is a condition that occurs when a diabetic has low blood glucose levels. (In Greek "hypo" means low; "glyc" refers to blood glucose; and "emia" refers to blood.) The most common cause of hypoglycemia is too much insulin. The insulin is taking away too much glucose from the blood. This is sometimes called an insulin reaction. A person experienc-ing hypoglycemia might feel shaky, cold and clammy, or hungry, or have a fast heartbeat. If he or she does not get glucose quickly, the condition will worsen. Dizziness, confu-sion, blurred vision, trouble walking and talking, a headache, and stomach cramps can set in. Someone with hypoglycemia can have all or just some of these symptoms. The worse the hypoglycemia gets, the worse the symptoms get. In extreme cases of hypoglycemia, a person can lose consciousness. This is called insulin shock. If someone is in insulin shock, he or she needs help from a doctor right away.

Often eating or drinking something with carbohydrates in it will ease the hypoglycemia. Some people drink fruit juice or eat a piece of hard candy. The sugar in the juice or candy raises the amount of glucose in the bloodstream. Many diabetics carry a supply of glucose tablets or glucose gel. These can be taken by mouth when the blood glucose gets low. After raising the carbohydrate level, it is important for the diabetic to do a blood test to check his or her blood glucose level.

HYPERGLYCEMIA

Hyperglycemia occurs when the blood glucose level is too high. (In Greek "hyper" means high.) The most common reason someone with diabetes has too much glucose is a lack of insulin. Without insulin, the body cannot move glucose from the bloodstream into cells. As a result, the blood glucose level becomes dangerously high. When a diabetic's glucose level is too high, the kidneys work harder to try to get rid of the extra glucose. Since the kidneys dispose of the extra glucose through urine, a hyperglycemic person has to go to the bathroom very often. This loss of fluids also leads to increased thirst. When someone with diabetes is hyperglycemic, he or she may have extreme thirst, frequent urination, and loss of

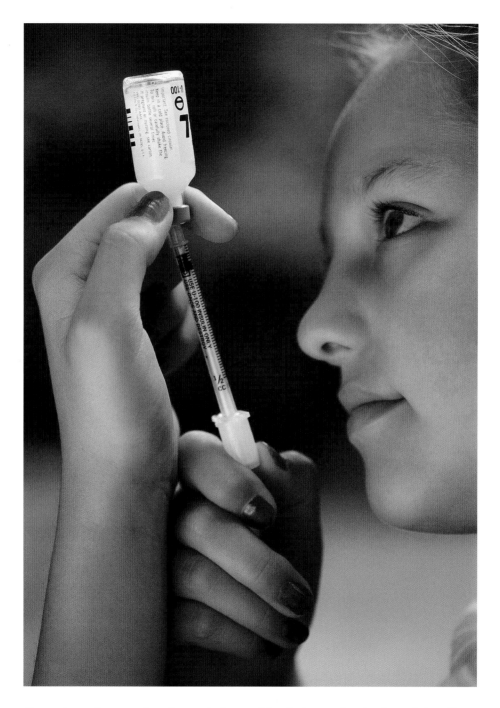

Hyperglycemics can often lower their own blood glucose levels through insulin injections. Sometimes hyperglycemia requires medical attention.

appetite. To treat hyperglycemia, the patient must bring his or her insulin levels back to normal. This is done through insulin injections.

KETOACIDOSIS

Cells that do not get energy from glucose use stored fat and protein to make the needed energy. When the body uses stored fat, it produces **ketone**. Soon, the bloodstream has too much ketone in it. Large amounts of ketone in the blood cause the blood to become acidic. This means there is too much acid in the blood. Acid in large quantities is poisonous. This condition is called **ketoacidosis**.

Over time, diabetics with severe hyperglycemia can suffer from ketoacidosis. Diabetics with ketoacidosis might be extremely thirsty and go to the bathroom very often. They might feel very sleepy, or have a hard time catching their breath. Their breath might have a sweet odor. Ketoacidosis is relatively easy to diagnose. Diabetics who think they might have ketoacidosis can do a urine test to see how much ketone is present. When a diabetic has ketoacidosis, he or she needs immediate medical attention. A healthcare professional will usually treat the condition with the necessary amounts of insulin and fluids. Sometimes a person

Different Types of Diabetes

There are two main forms of diabetes: diabetes insipidus and diabetes mellitus. Diabetes insipidus is a disease that has to do with the kidneys' inability to retain, or keep, enough water. Diabetes mellitus involves the body's insulin and glucose maintenance.

There are three different types of diabetes mellitus. Juvenile diabetes—sometimes called Type 1 diabetes—is one form of the disease. Type 2 diabetes is similar to juvenile diabetes, but develops in adults. Many doctors believe that hereditary factors, being overweight, and having a poor diet that is high in sugars can lead to Type 2 diabetes. But most Type 2 diabetics can manage the disease through medication, proper diet, and exercise. The third form of diabetes mellitus is gestational diabetes. Women sometimes develop the disease during pregnancy. But this type of diabetes mellitus usually goes away after the baby is born. However, women who had gestational diabetes are at greater risk for developing Type 2 diabetes. With proper treatment, diabetics—regardless of their form or type of diabetes—can live normal healthy lives.

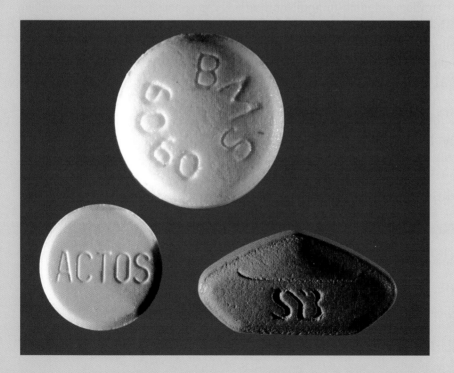

Different types of medication in pill form can be used to treat Type 2 diabetes.

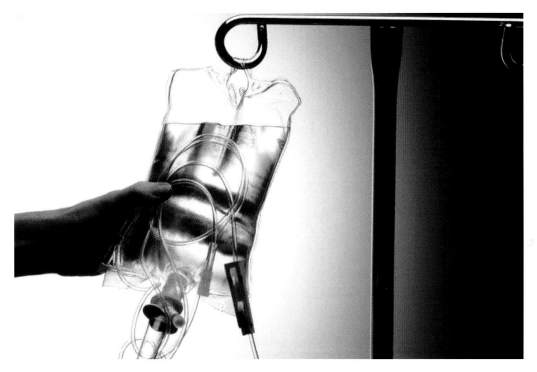

Intravenous fluids—also known as IV fluids—are often used to treat ketoacidosis. These fluids enter the body through blood vessels.

with ketoacidosis needs to spend some time in the hospital to ensure that his or her glucose level goes back to normal.

HOW DOES A PERSON GET JUVENILE DIABETES?

People used to think that diabetes was caused by eating and drinking too much. A healthy pancreas can make enough insulin to handle a lot of sugar. If someone does eat too much sugar, it is usually stored in the body as fat. This can be unhealthy, but it does not cause juvenile diabetes. (Obesity—being overweight—and a diet high in sugar may

The immune system usually fights off viruses—shown here, magnified by an electron microscope. But sometimes viruses like these can cause changes in the response of the immune system, resulting in diseases such as juvenile diabetes.

cause a different type of diabetes.) This disease is not contagious. A person cannot "catch" juvenile diabetes like a cold.

Scientists do know that diabetes is a hereditary disease. This means that if someone in a family has diabetes, other people in that family have a greater chance of developing the disease. But this does not necessarily mean that other members of the diabetic's family will definitely develop diabetes. In fact, studies have shown that if one identical twin has juvenile diabetes, the other twin only has a 30 to 50 percent chance of getting it, too.

Juvenile diabetes is an **autoimmune disease.** When a foreign substance is in the body, the immune system is trained to attack it. This is good for illnesses like the flu. The immune system works to kill the flu virus. But in juvenile diabetes, the immune system has attacked harmless cells that are supposed to make insulin. This results in decreased insulin production. It can take anywhere from a few months to a few years for these cells to stop making insulin. This is why a child may not appear to have juvenile diabetes right after he or she is born. The disease may take years to develop.

Scientists do not know why the body thinks the insulin-making cells are invaders. One theory is that viruses may cause a self-directed immune response. This happens when the body gets confused about which cells are its own and which are the foreign cells that it should be fighting. But this is just a theory—scientists are not sure if it is true.

Though many questions about juvenile diabetes are still unanswered, great progress has been made. Thanks to many years of research, medical professionals today have a better understanding of this disease. This knowledge has helped to create better ways to diagnose and treat diabetic patients, extending the length and quality of their lives.

3

THE HISTORY OF DIABETES

Though modern methods of diagnosis and treatment have been developed within the last few decades, scientists and physicians have studied diabetes for more than a thousand years. Over time, new developments in technology have helped, but nearly everything known about diabetes today is built on the important diabetes discoveries made years ago.

In ancient Egypt, people did not call this disease "diabetes," but many still suffered from it. In the year 1552 B.C.E., an Egyptian doctor named Hesy-Ra examined a patient who had to go to the bathroom often. Hesy-Ra did not know what was causing the illness, but he thought that a special diet might help. The foods Hesy-Ra suggested for the diet were fruits, grains, and honey. The diet helped—but did not cure the patient.

This wooden panel of Hesy-Ra was created in Egypt.

A Not-So-Sweet Job

....

Since Hesy-Ra's time, most doctors have known that diabetics have a lot of sugar in their urine. As a result, doctors felt that testing the urine for sugar was one way to diagnose diabetes. Today, doctors still do urine testing, but they are lucky enough to have special chemical tests. Doctors—and their assistants—of the past were not so fortunate. Until the eleventh century, a different method for testing urine was used. Doctors hired assistants to work as tasters. These tasters would tell the doctor if the urine was sweet. If it was, the doctor assumed that the patient had diabetes.

Around the same time, doctors in China and India saw patients with similar problems. Like Hesy-Ra, these doctors did not know how to treat the illness. Indian doctors thought that their patients were eating and drinking too much and had them reduce their food intake.

Around 100 to 175 C.E., doctors started calling this disease diabetes. Historians are not sure who chose the name, but it might have been Galen of Pergamum, Apollonius of Memphis, or Aretaeus of Cappadocia. All of these men were Greek doctors. The disease received its name from a patient's frequent need to urinate. The word "diabetes" comes from the Greek word for "siphon." A siphon is a tube that is used to drain liquids. The Latin word for honey, "mellitus," was later added to help describe the fact that a diabetic's urine contained a lot of sugar. As a result, the full name of one kind of diabetes is diabetes mellitus. Even though scientists at that time learned new things about the disease, and could give it a name, diabetes remained a serious problem without any effective treatment and many people died from it.

CHANGING DIETS

In the early 1800s, scientists were able to use chemicals to measure sugar in the urine. During the 1870s, a French doctor named Apollinaire Bouchardat found that some of his diabetic patients had less sugar in their urine. He was not sure why at first, but then realized that his patients' diets had changed. At that time, France was at war with Germany and there was less food to go around. People were eating less than they had before the war. Bouchardat decided that people with diabetes did much better if they did not eat as much. He told his patients to start eating less. The diets helped, but patients still had the disease and continued to develop serious problems.

Sometimes the diet prescribed by the doctor was almost as bad as the disease. One French doctor who lived in the late 1800s told people with diabetes to eat extra large helpings of sugar. He thought that the patient needed to replace all of the sugar the body lost in the urine. In the years that followed, many diabetic patients around the world began to follow diets made up of just one kind of food. For example, some people ate only cereal or oatmeal. Some followed the "milk diet," or the "rice cure." Others were told that their meals could only be made of potatoes. Many diabetics were treated using a dangerous drug made from poppy seeds. Not many people enjoyed these diets. One doctor who lived in Italy had to lock up his patients while he was treating them. He found that it was the only way that he could get them to stick to the strict diet. Unfortunately, these diets did not usually work over a long period of time. All of these experiments, however, taught scientists more about the disease.

INSULIN, SUGAR, AND THE PANCREAS

In 1889, two Austrian scientists, Oskar Minkowski and Joseph von Mering, decided to find out what part the pancreas played in digestion. To do that, they removed the pancreas from a dog. Without a pancreas, the dog developed diabetes. That is how doctors discovered that the pancreas was connected to diabetes. But they still did not know how to treat diabetes.

Newer diabetes discoveries continued to be made. Georg Zuelzer, a scientist living in Germany, worked on treatments for diabetics. In 1908 he gave his patients shots of a fluid he had taken from a human pancreas. The shot helped reduce the amount of sugar in the urine, but it also made the patients very sick.

About the same time that Dr. Zuelzer was treating his patients, a doctor named Frederick Madison Allen was making more discoveries in the United States. Dr. Allen observed at least one hundred diabetic patients in order to come to his conclusions about diabetes. He also opened a clinic in New Jersey that treated illnesses such as diabetes. Dr. Allen called one of his discoveries "Allen's Law," and he wrote a book about it. The law said that if a healthy person without diabetes is given a large amount of sugar, the body uses up the sugar. But giving more sugar to a diabetic means that more sugar will be excreted—moved out of the body— through urine. Allen's Law was another step toward finding helpful treatments for diabetics.

In 1920 a Canadian named Frederick Banting was experiment-ing with different types of fluids taken from the pancreas of a dog. He and his associates—C. H. Best, J. B. Collip, and J. J. R. Macleod—then injected the fluids into dogs that had their pancreases removed. One of the fluids brought the dogs' blood glucose levels under control. The pancreatic fluid that they used was insulin.

By January of 1922, the scientists were ready to give insulin to their first human diabetic, an eleven-year-old boy

Canadian scientist Frederick Banting

from Toronto named Leonard Thompson. The insulin they gave him was derived from cows. After he received the shot, Leonard Thompson began to get healthier. His blood glucose level was closer to normal. He began to eat a more normal diet, and he gained weight. The treatment was considered a success.

Five months later, a company started to produce this type of insulin in large quantities. This meant that doctors all over the world could use it to treat diabetes. In 1923, Dr. Banting and Dr. Macleod were given the Nobel Prize in Medicine for their use of insulin to treat diabetics. In the 1920s scientists continued to find ways to make large quantities of insulin for diabetic treatments.

In 1925, Dr. E. M. K. Gelling ran experiments in his laboratory at Johns Hopkins University in Maryland. He was looking for a way to produce insulin in large quantities.

MORE MEDICAL BREAKTHROUGHS

In the 1950s scientists developed more medicine that helped control blood glucose levels. This medicine could be taken orally, which meant it could be swallowed in pill or liquid

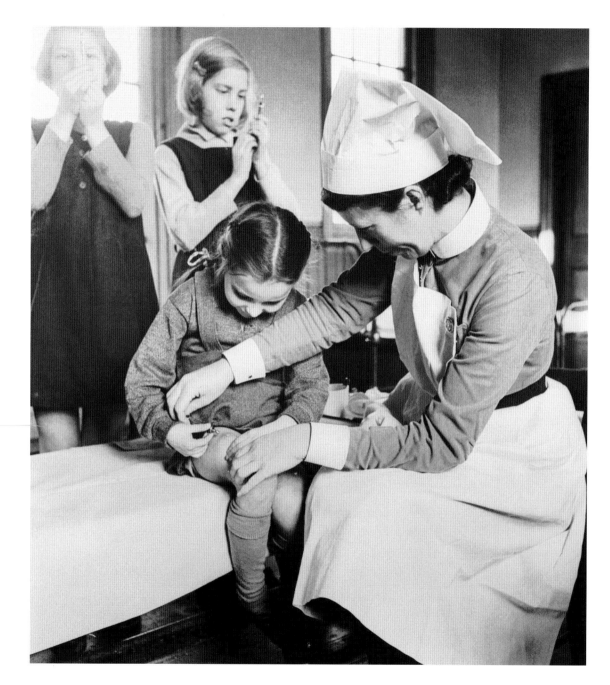

In the late 1940s, children diagnosed with juvenile diabetes started to learn how to give themselves insulin injections.

form. Scientists working during the 1960s invented a test that allowed people to test the sugar in their urine at home. Before this, a diabetic patient frequently went to his doctor's office or to a hospital to be tested. By testing for sugar themselves, diabetic patients could tell how much insulin they needed to take. During the 1970s laboratories developed tests that measured the amount of glucose in a patient's blood.

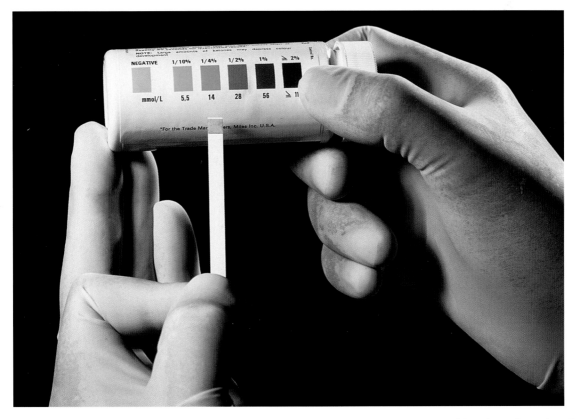

Chemicals in urinalysis test strips change color when they come into contact with urine. The colored strip can then be compared to a chart that lists glucose levels by color.

Yeast that has been altered to produce human insulin is grown in special vessels in laboratories.

Glucose measurements taken from the blood tend to be more accurate than measurements taken from urine. This is because a blood glucose test shows how much glucose is in the blood at the time of the test, allowing a patient to figure out how much medicine is needed at that time. All of these break-throughs helped diabetics take a more active role in controlling their diabetes.

A huge insulin-related breakthrough occurred in the 1980s. In 1983 the first biosynthetic human insulin was used on diabetics. Biosynthetic insulin is not found in nature and has been made in laboratories. It is identical to natural human insulin. Scientists found a way to produce this artificial insulin in large quantities. **Bacteria** and yeast cells were genetically changed so that they would produce this human-like insulin. Factories could then use huge vats—or contain-ers—to grow millions of insulin-producing cells. Through the years researchers have found that it is easier to control the quality and purity of the bacteria- or yeast-made insulin. Cow and pig insulin were not always safe to use. Diseases and other problems associated with cows and pigs could cause impurities in the insulin, making diabetics who used it sick. Most diabetics now use the biosynthetic version.

As insulin production improved, newer methods to

A scientist at the National Institutes of Health in Maryland uses a laser scan microscope to do her diabetes research.

administer the insulin were also developed. In the past doctors only used traditional syringes and vials—or bottles—of insulin. The needle of the syringe is inserted into the bottle and the correct amount of insulin is withdrawn. The patient is then injected with the insulin. This method is still used, but now there are other alternatives available. All syringes and needles used to inject insulin (and other medicines) are disposable. This prevents the spread of infection and disease. Newer types of needles and syringes have been invented to make the injections less painful. Many insulin kits are small and easy to carry around. Scientists have also built portable pumps that can automatically deliver insulin.

Someday scientists hope to find a way to cure diabetes or at least find more convenient ways to treat it. No one knows for sure when such developments may occur, but without the creativity and determination of past and present diabetes researchers—and their patients—such progress would be impossible.

4

LIVING WITH JUVENILE DIABETES

Despite the years of research and discovery, there is no cure for juvenile diabetes. Diabetics must understand the disease, how it affects them, and how they can manage their lives around it. Dealing with juvenile diabetes can be scary and overwhelming at first, but there are many people who understand and can help. The American Diabetes Association estimates that there are 500,000 to 1 million children with juvenile diabetes living in the United States. Nearly every city or town has support groups to help diabetics and their families. People who attend these group sessions include doctors and other healthcare professionals, diabetics, and relatives of diabetics. These people have had experience with the disease and can offer information, advice, or emotional support. Hospitals, health centers, and schools often have informational sessions about diabetes. Learning about the disease is one of the first steps toward managing it.

TREATMENT

Besides understanding the disease, managing juvenile diabetes also includes being health-conscious. Juvenile diabetes can be treated through glucose monitoring, insulin therapy, a well-balanced diet, and regular exercise.

Glucose Testing and Monitoring

Blood glucose monitoring means watching how blood glucose levels change over time. People with juvenile diabetes must test the amount of glucose in their blood a few times each day. Usually diabetics test their blood glucose level before taking insulin injections, eating, exercising, or going to sleep. Through glucose testing they will know if the level is too high, too low, or just right.

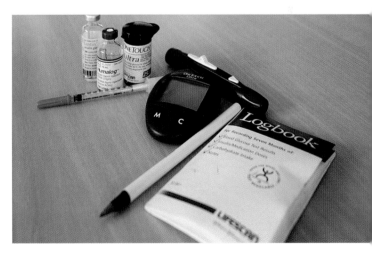

Blood glucose monitoring involves a variety of tools.

Patients with juvenile diabetes use special equipment to test their blood glucose level. This includes a glucose testing machine called a **blood glucose meter,** and a lancing device and **lancets.** The blood glucose meter is a machine that tests for glucose and displays how much glucose is in the blood. The test is relatively painless and after performing it several times, many diabetics can do it quickly and easily.

The first step is getting a blood sample. Only a very small amount of blood is needed for the test, so diabetics use small needles called lancets and a lancing device. The device guides the lancet into the skin. Lancing devices come in many shapes and forms. Some are pen shaped, while others are small and oblong. Whatever their size or shape, lancing devices are built in a way that

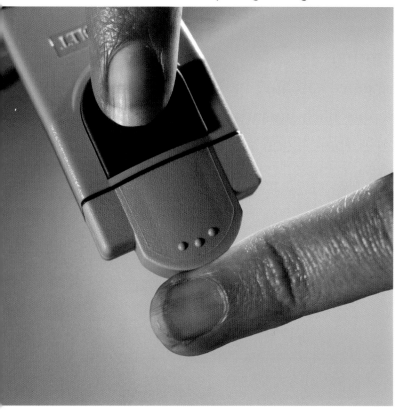

Most lancing devices are small and easy to handle.

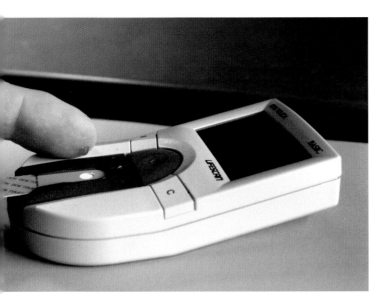

Some glucose meters require squeezing a drop of blood onto the test strips. Many diabetics use glucose meter strips that are lightly pressed against the blood on the skin.

pricks the skin just enough to get the right amount of blood. Most diabetics take their blood samples from their fingertips, though some also get blood from areas on their arms or legs.

After the lancet is used and a drop of blood appears on the skin, the blood is put onto a test strip. The test strip is a piece of paper treated with certain chemicals that respond to the glucose in the blood. The blood glucose meter then reads the test strip to determine the amount of blood glucose. (Some glucose meters have the test strip attached to the device, while others require inserting the unattached test strip into the meter.) The glucose meter takes anywhere from a few seconds to one minute to measure the glucose. When the blood glucose meter has finished reading the blood on the test strip, it will display the blood glucose level on the screen.

Most people with diabetes keep a record, or log, of their test results. The glucose log can be helpful to the doctors treating a person with diabetes. A doctor can see if the patient is improving or needs to have his or her medicine adjusted. The log also helps a diabetic become familiar with what time of day he or she is most likely to have low or high blood glucose levels. Knowing when blood glucose is usually low or high can help a diabetic plan snacks, meals, and activities. Most importantly, keeping track of glucose levels helps to determine the amount and type of medicine the diabetic needs.

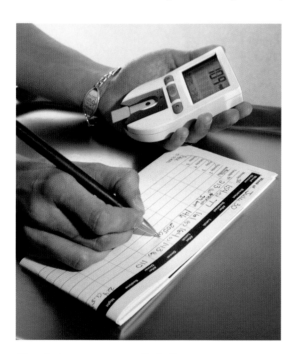

Blood glucose meters digitally display the blood glucose measurement, making it easier for a diabetic to record the data.

Insulin Therapy

To maintain proper blood glucose levels, most juvenile diabetics undergo insulin therapy. This therapy involves adding specific amounts of insulin into the blood. Insulin is made in laboratories and comes in three main types:

Glucose Testing Safety

To prevent infections and other illnesses there are a few safety rules to follow with blood glucose testing.

• Before drawing blood, make sure the skin is clean. Most people use alcohol wipes to prepare the area.

• After testing always put the cap back on the lancet and dispose of it properly. Lancets should not be thrown away in the regular trash. A health professional can explain where a diabetic can dispose of the lancets.

• A diabetic should only use his or her own lancets and blood glucose meter.

Used lancets and needles should be thrown away in the appropriate medical waste container.

short acting, intermediate acting, and long acting. The difference between these three types is how long the insulin dose lasts before another dose is needed. For each diabetic, a doctor decides which kind of insulin works best, what amounts of insulin are needed, and how often the insulin should be administered.

The insulin must be injected into the fat tissue right under the skin. The most common places on the body for insulin injections are the stomach, buttock, outer thigh, and upper arm. Some diabetics use a syringe and a container of insulin, measuring out the proper dosage each time. Others use

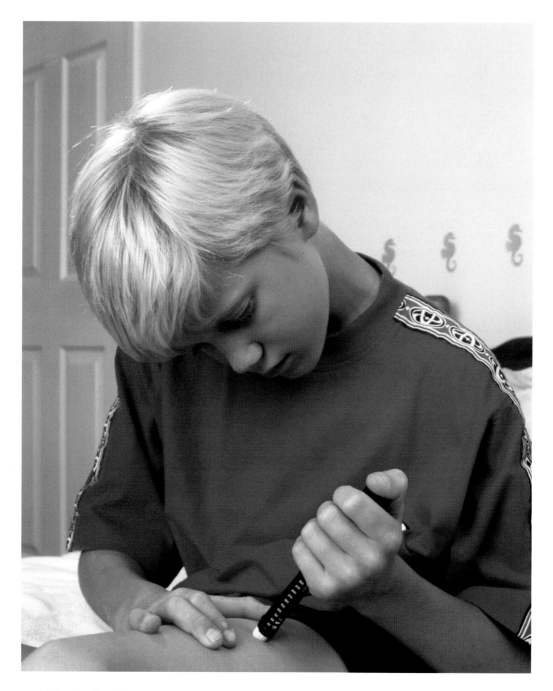

Many diabetics find it easier to use a pen-like insulin injector that uses insulin cartridges.

injectors which contain pre-measured cartridges of insulin. Many injectors are pen shaped, making them easy to store, hold, and use. The needles for insulin injections are very small and go into the skin very easily. After a while, insulin injections can be almost painless.

Today, many people with diabetes use **insulin pumps.** An insulin pump is carried outside the body on a special belt or in a person's pocket. The pump is about the size of a pager. It is connected to a flexible plastic tube attached to a needle. The needle is inserted under the skin in the abdominal area. The pump

An insulin cartridge is loaded into a small insulin pump.

delivers small amounts of insulin throughout the day and night. Diabetics can program the pumps to give more insulin at specific times, such as before meals. People with insulin pumps do not need to give themselves insulin injections. But insulin pumps are not right for everyone. By taking into account his or her age, habits, and lifestyle, a diabetic and his or her doctor can decide if the insulin pump is the best choice.

Scientists are currently working on new ways to administer insulin. Unfortunately, insulin cannot be taken by mouth—in liquid or pill form—because the stomach's digestive process would destroy it. But many laboratories are working on ways to make a pill that can withstand digestion, and deliver the insulin efficiently. Other scientists are trying to find a way to make insulin that can be inhaled. Rather than injecting the medicine, a diabetic could breathe in a special powder. Special patches that allow the skin to absorb the insulin are also being tested.

Researchers are also experimenting with an artificial pancreas. Parts of this device would be implanted within a diabetic's body. The artificial organ would function the way a healthy pancreas should. It could keep track of the blood glucose and deliver the correct amount of insulin. This way no additional insulin—in pill, liquid, patch, or injection form—would be needed. Progress continues to be made toward realizing these advancements, but more research and testing still needs to be done.

Parts of the artificial pancreas are surgically inserted into the body, while the rest is worn on a belt or clipped to clothing. The artificial pancreas can automatically test and regulate insulin levels.

The Diabetes Kit

Diabetics should always carry a special kit of supplies that help with diabetes treatment. This kit should include the following:

- A medical alert card stating that he or she has diabetes. (Some diabetics wear a special medical ID necklace or bracelet.)
- Glucose testing supplies
- Carbohydrate-rich snacks to correct low blood glucose
- Insulin to correct hyperglycemia

Medical alert tags are important for times when a diabetic is unable to tell a paramedic about his or her diabetes.

Eating Well

Eating a well-balanced diet is very important to the health of people with juvenile diabetes. The right foods can help keep the blood glucose level stable. The body needs carbohydrates for energy, so it is important that a person with diabetes gets a moderate amount of carbohydrates. A "moderate amount" means not too much and not too little. This will help glucose levels stay as close to normal as possible.

Many people think that sugar is never allowed in the diet of a person with diabetes. But this is not always true. Foods like pasta and sugary foods like chocolate contain carbohydrates. The difference is that one serving of chocolate has more carbohydrates than one serving of pasta. Also, pasta has nutrients that are good for the body. Even though pasta is probably a better choice, eating a small amount of chocolate might not cause harm to a person with diabetes. But each diabetic is different, so he or she must listen to a doctor's instructions and follow the prescribed diet.

Diabetics need to be careful about foods with large amounts of starch, such as pasta and bread.

Exercise

Exercising regularly is important for everybody. It lowers the risk of heart disease and can help a person control his or her weight. But exercise is really good for people with diabetes. When the body is active, it must use more glucose for energy to keep going. Exercise therefore lowers the amount of glucose in the bloodstream.

Everyone should do some physical activity to keep in shape. Children with juvenile diabetes should talk to their doctors about the right amount and type of exercise.

It is very important for diabetics to discuss exercise with their doctors. Since exercise lowers the blood glucose level, the amount of insulin a person needs to inject can change. A doctor must calculate the right insulin dosage. If a diabetic begins exercising without first speaking with a doctor, the insulin doses could be incorrect, causing more medical problems.

Famous Diabetics

Some of the most successful athletes, inventors, politicians, and artists managed to cope with diabetes. Working alongside many dedicated individuals, these famous people often raise funds for and call attention to the need for more diabetes research and awareness. Famous diabetics include

Thomas Edison, inventor
Mary Tyler Moore, actress
Bobby Clarke, NHL player, coach, and member of the Hockey Hall of Fame
Charles "Buddy" Roemer, former governor and U.S. Representative
Larry King, television talk show host

Zippora Karz, New York City Ballet dancer
Chris Dudley, NBA center
Michelle McGann, professional golfer
Ken Anderson, NFL quarterback and coach
Nicole Johnson, Miss America 1999
B.B. King, musician

Having diabetes did not prevent Thomas Edison (left), Bobby Clarke (center), or Mary Tyler Moore (right) from pursuing their dreams. Moore now serves as the international chairwoman for the Juvenile Diabetes Research Foundation.

COMPLICATIONS

If diabetes goes untreated or if a diabetic does not monitor glucose levels, many problems—or complications—can occur.

Microvascular Complications. "Micro" means small and "vascular" refers to the blood vessels, so microvascular complications involve damage to a person's small blood vessels. The main microvascular problem people with diabetes can develop is eye damage. Parts of the human eye have tiny fragile blood vessels that, over time, can be damaged by high levels of glucose in the blood. Blindness can sometimes occur in severe cases of diabetes. As a result, diabetics should see an eye doctor, or ophthalmologist, regularly.

Macrovascular Complications. "Macro" means large, so macrovascular damage affects large blood vessels. Veins and arteries are large blood vessels that can be affected by diabetes. A diabetic may have changes in the way blood flows—or circulates—throughout the body. Diabetics have an increased risk of heart disease and stroke. (A stroke occurs when the brain does not receive enough blood.) The flow of blood to the legs and feet can be damaged, too. Because these potential problems may occur, doctors carefully monitor a diabetic's circulation.

Neuropathy. People with diabetes may also experience

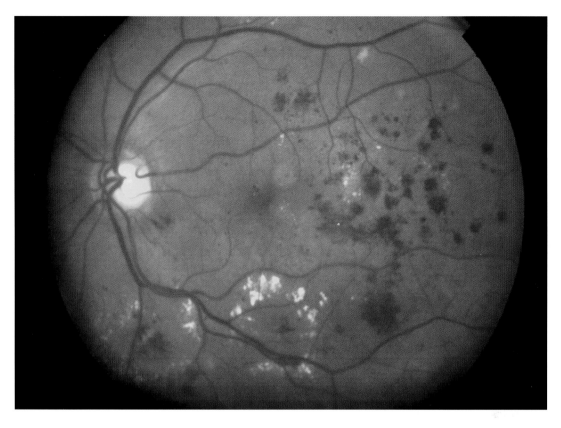

The human eye has many thin blood vessels. These delicate blood vessels can be damaged from complications associated with diabetes.

nerve damage, which is called neuropathy ("neuro" means nerve and "pathy" means disease). Nerves are bundles of fibers found throughout the human body. Nerve cells are responsible for receiving and sending messages between the brain and other parts of the body through these fibers. There are many kinds of nerve damage, and they can affect

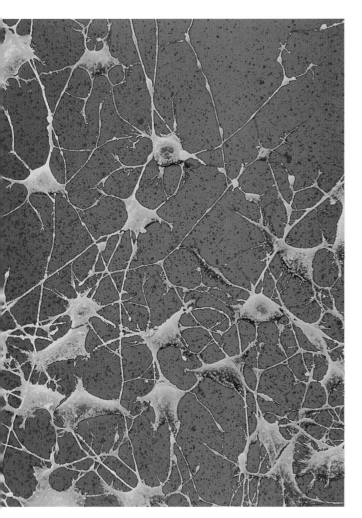

A colored electron micrograph of healthy nerve cells.

different regions of the body. When nerve damage occurs, some diabetics have sensitive skin, leg cramps, or numbness or tingling in the toes and feet. Neuropathy is a possible complication of diabetes, but it takes a long time to develop.

Nephropathy. This diabetic complication involves the kidneys ("nephro" means kidney and "pathy" means disease). The job of the kidneys is to keep the body clean. They do this by using **nephrons** that filter toxic material that is harmful to the body. Diabetes can damage the nephrons, allowing harmful material to circulate around the body, causing illness. The kidneys have many nephrons, so serious problems only occur when about 80 percent of the nephrons have been damaged. Nephropathy is very serious and can lead to kidney failure. When the kidneys stop

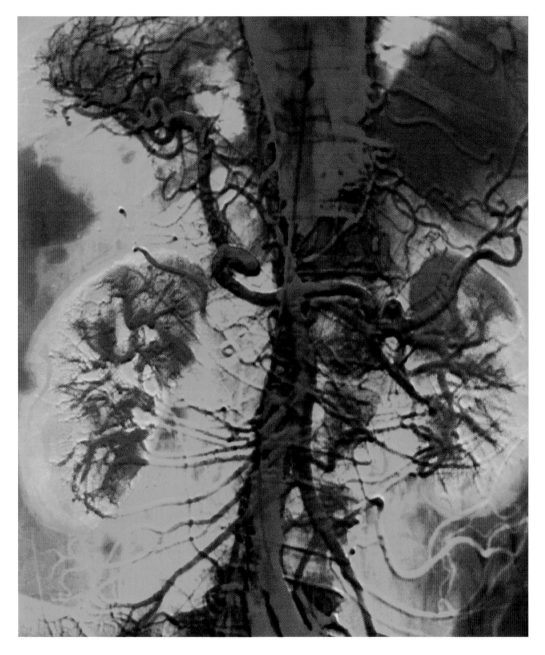

Nearly all humans are born with two kidneys, shown in yellow in this x-ray.

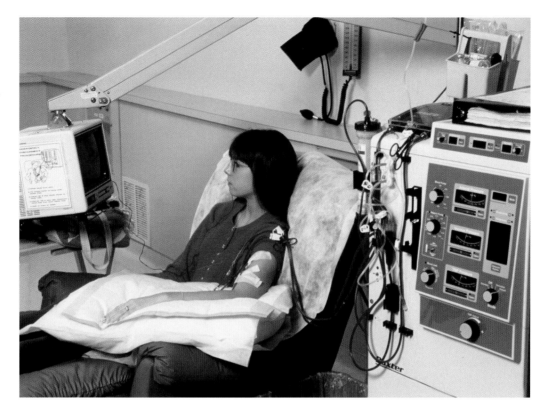

When a person's kidneys no longer function properly, a dialysis machine is sometimes used to filter the blood.

working—or fail—a person must undergo a treatment called **dialysis.** This treatment is performed regularly and cleans the body of toxic material. Many people on dialysis eventually require kidney transplants.

It is important to remember that not all people with diabetes will have all of these problems. Some of these complications can be delayed or prevented by practicing

To stay healthy, people of all ages should visit their doctor for regular exams.

good diabetes control. This means that a diabetic must keep his or her blood glucose level as close to normal as possible, eat right, exercise correctly, and follow doctors' instructions. Understanding the disease and taking control can help to ensure a healthy life.

GLOSSARY

autoimmune disease—A condition in which the body attacks its own normal healthy cells.

bacteria—Very small living cells which can only be seen using a microscope.

blood glucose—The amount of glucose in the bloodstream.

blood glucose meter—A device that measures the amount of glucose in the bloodstream.

carbohydrates—Chemical compounds found in food. Starch and sugars are carbohydrates used to make glucose.

dialysis—A treatment for kidney failure that cleans the body of toxic material.

glucose—A type of sugar.

glucose level—The amount of sugar in the bloodstream.

hormones—Chemicals that help body functions.

hyperglycemia—The condition in which blood glucose levels are high.

hypoglycemia—The condition in which blood glucose levels are low.

insulin—The hormone that helps to turn blood sugar into energy.

insulin pump—A pager-sized device that delivers insulin to a diabetic throughout the day.

islets of Langerhans—Small cells that secrete insulin. These cells are found in the pancreas.

ketoacidosis—The condition in which blood has too many ketones, causing the blood to be very acidic.

ketone—A substance created when the body uses stored fat as a source of energy.

kidneys—The internal organs that remove toxic substances from the body.

lancet—A needle used to prick the skin during a blood glucose test.

macrovascular—A term that refers to large blood vessels.

microvascular—A term that refers to small blood vessels.

metabolize—To change substances in the body in order to create new materials or energy.

nephrons—The structures in the kidneys that filter toxins.

nephropathy—A complication of diabetes that affects the kidneys.

neuropathy—A complication of diabetes that affects nerves.

pancreas—The internal organ (located behind the stomach in humans) that makes insulin.

virus—A small particle that can cause illness or disease.

FIND OUT MORE

These two diabetes organizations have chapters—or groups—in nearly every state. You can visit their Web sites or call their toll-free numbers to find the chapters closest to you.

Diabetes Organizations

The Juvenile Diabetes Research Foundation International
120 Wall Street
New York, NY 10005
1-800-533-CURE
www.jdf.org

The American Diabetes Association
1701 North Beauregard Street
Alexandria, VA 22311
1-800-DIABETES
www.diabetes.org

Books

American Diabetes Association. *American Diabetes Association Complete Guide to Diabetes: The Ultimate Home Reference from the Diabetes Experts, 3rd Edition*. New York: McGraw-Hill/Contemporary Distributed Products, 2002.

American Diabetes Association. *Diabetes A to Z, 5th Edition*. Virginia: American Diabetes Association, 2003.

Geil, Patti Bazel, and Tami A. Ross. *Cooking up Fun for Kids with Diabetes*. New York: McGraw-Hill/Contemporary Distributed Products, 2003.

Gray, Shirley Wimbish. *Living With Diabetes*. Chanhassen, MN: Child's World, 2003.

Loy, Spike Nasmyth. *Getting a Grip on Diabetes: Quick Tips for Kids and Teens*. Alexandria, VA: American Diabetes Association, 2000.

Mazur, Marcia Levine, and Peter Banks. *The Dinosaur Tamer and Other Stories for Children with Diabetes*. New York: McGraw-Hill/Contemporary Distributed Products, 1996.

Peacock, Carol Antoinette, and Adair Gregory, and Kyle Carney Gregory. *Sugar Was My Best Food: Diabetes and Me*. Morton Grove, IL: Whitman, 1998.

Silverstein, Alvin, Virginia Silverstein, and Laura Silverstein Nunn. *Diabetes*. Danbury, CT: Franklin Watts, 2002.

Stewart, Gail B. *Diabetes*. San Diego, CA: Kidhaven Press, 2003.

Thomas, Maria, and Loren W. Grene. *The Unofficial Guide to Living with Diabetes*. New York: Macmillan, 1999.

Web Sites

American Diabetes Association Wizdom Youth Zone
http://web.diabetes.org/wizdom/index.shtml

Canadian Diabetes Association
http://www.diabetes.ca/Section_about/index.asp

Centers for Disease Control and Prevention: Diabetes Public
Health Resource
http://www.cdc.gov/diabetes

Children's Diabetes Foundation
http://www.childrensdiabetesfdn.com/index.htm

Children with DIABETES—Children's Corner
http://www.childrenwithdiabetes.com/kids/

Defeat Diabetes Foundation
http://www.defeatdiabetes.org

Diabetes Exercise and Sports Association
www.diabetes-exercise.org

International Diabetes Federation
http://www.idf.org/home

JDRF Kids Online
http://kids.jdrf.org

Joslin Diabetes Center
http://www.joslin.harvard.edu/news/helping_kidsfamily.shtml

National Diabetes Information Clearinghouse (NDIC)
http://diabetes.niddk.nih.gov

INDEX

ABOUT THE AUTHOR

Johannah Haney has been interested in juvenile diabetes since she grew up with a close friend who has the disease. When they were younger, they used to attend a special diabetes summer camp together. Haney is now a writer living in Boston, Massachusetts. She has written several textbooks and articles for magazines.